The Journey to Discover Your True Self

K. M. Chalebgwa

Copyright © 2011 by K. Maggie Chalebgwa

All rights reserved. Written permission must be secured from the publisher to use or reproduce any part of this book, except for brief quotation in critical review or articles.

Published by Horizon designs and Printing
P.O. Box 403301 Gaborone
Tel: 0267 3947326

ISBN: 978-99912-940-1-8

The work of this book is dedicated
to the memory of my brother
Mothomotho-Square.

We can only measure the success of
our life by what we donate to it.

Acknowledgements

Special thanks goes to Daniel Mashimbye for taking part in the journey with me providng support during difficult times. He gave me the courage to on go on even when it seemed the ship was sinking.

CONTENTS

PREFACE

From birth to death life is full of experiences, some good and some bad. To some it may seem it is better to be dead than be alive; to others life experiences bring joy, and is better to be alive than to die.

This book is for those who want to make choices on their life journey. The truth lies in your true self. This book will help you discover your true self.

What I want to share with readers is a journey through the inner self so that you get to appreciate the challenges you have to overcome in order to realize your potential. There is no one path or technique that will lead you to your true self. Nevertheless, by attending to what goes on inside of you, you affect your lifestyle and adopt new habits that will see you understand yourself better. Habits are consistent thoughts, actions and deeds. It is habits that nourish the goodness in us that inspire us to reach higher levels and create better opportunities.

Those who go on the journey to find who they are will enjoy benefits that include overall satisfaction with their lives as they grow to focus better on their career development, are generally appreciative and get to enjoy what they do and relate well with family, colleagues and friends.

This book allows you to realize that you hold the power and the key to your future. Only you can open the doors that will release the best of you. Take this journey that will enable you to gain new perspective that will help you make sense of life experiences. The confidence you gain on this journey will help you make choices that will get you closer to where you want to go.

INTRODUCTION

Accountability is the best place to start the journey. Making your life count is simply to help you build yourself starting with what you have. Defining the best in your journey is that you count on you first – you depend on what is inside of you. Potential, confidence, success, growth, etc. is all in the space you occupy in life.

Confidence allows you to perform better in your own space. Millions of people lack confidence because of lack of accountability to themselves. The lack of confidence is highly associated with lack of accountability. The chapters in this book are put together to help you to take charge of your life and develop more skills to become competent.

The journey of life starts with the first step, it starts the day you were born and you start directing it when you make the first deliberate decision to travel towards a specific destination.

On this journey you start making choices. You choose to go out in the first place; you make choices as you reach crossroads. If you do not know where you want to go, then any road you follow is 'ok' – your journey will be senseless, you will still reach some destination even if it is not where you might have wanted to be. You can choose to know where you are going.

Use the chapters in this book to become skilled, understanding yourself – your strengths and capabilities to embrace your destiny. You owe it to yourself to make the best of your life, to take control of your life and find your own space in life. Let the journey begin.

1

Make your life count

It is easier to be yourself than to try to be what other people want you to be. On being yourself, you conform only to your wishes and desires; you take advantage of your strengths as you find fit; you work towards your desired goals and never those handed to you by others; you respond to your needs and make use of all the resources available to you without waiting for others to decide for you. Only you know where you want to go, and it is only you who can get you there.

> Relying on others to decide what you
> have to do with your life is going to limit
> you to only what they know and desire.

Sometimes we hand over the responsibility of our lives to others when we expect them to make decisions for us. Their choices may take us in any direction. They may choose that you be like them, but the reality is that you are an original, different from all others and capable of totally different achievements. One great artist once said, "My mother said to me, 'If you become a soldier you'll become a general, if you become a monk you'll end up as the pope.' Instead, I became a painter and wound up as Picasso." Had Picasso chosen to follow any of the common careers, the world will never have seen and enjoyed this great man's work. On being himself, he realised a completely new set of achievements which no one will ever do like him. Anyone who tries to imitate another person, would at best be second best.

By choosing to be like another person, you limit yourself to what their are. You even deny yourself the opportunity to define your guiding principles and values. In the end you can only be second best.

Deciding to be yourself is the first step towards fulfilling your potential, making real the dormant, still untapped capabilities of your hidden talents special only to you.

You first have to find yourself. Follow what you are good at. That will dominate your desires and unlock your potential. Your potential will remain dormant, until you choose to do something about getting the best out of yourself. Presently all your best qualities are buried deeply under, covered by the attitudes about yourself and assumptions you hold about what is expected of you.

In our formative years, we are told what to do and what not to do by our parents and teachers. Most of us grow up conforming to the set rules without daring to get out of step. On joining the workforce, this attitude is continued. Our bosses and colleagues keep us in check. In married life, most will do what is expected of them by their spouses. By this time you might have lost the spoteneity of doing what you think is right as well as your individuality, living your life through hopes and wishes of others. It finally reduces you to only a shell of what your life could have been. Your personality, strengths, abilities, talents and capabilities get buried under the meek, often prepared to please person you have grown to become.

Borrowing strength builds weakness. It builds weakness in the borrower because it reinforces dependence on external factors to get things done. It builds weakness in the person forced to acquiesce, stunting development of independent reasoning, growth and internal discipline.

- Stephen Covey

Most people around you prefer to see you conforming to imaginary rules, that are easy to predict. That is what they have grown to expect from those close and around them.

We all need to start looking at life differently and expecting more of ourselves. Give more of yourself so that you get to reap proportionately more. The level of excitement you enjoy is related to the personal fulfilment coming from fulfilling your dreams, not those of others.

Being yourself is easier in that it is sponteneous and does not involve learning rules to conform to what others want and expect.

To be yourself is not written anywhere for you to try to study before acting on it. It is exciting in that you get to do your heart's desire and can try out new things. Nevertheless, to get to fulfil your dream involves working on what you want. Your potential will remain untapped as long as you do not work on it. No great achievement will come to you without you first working on your dreams.

Each of us has something unique to the self to offer. Start with what you can do, taking advantage of your strengths, then make a deliberate effort to work on your weak points for improved output.

Never allow what you cannot do
stop you from going ahead. Use
what you can do to get there.

Enjoy the thrill of success through doing that which others think can never be done.

The thrill of stealing bases when playing baseball is because it gives you a chance to think quickly and put to test your running skill, all in the effort to beat the opposition. Otherwise you will never know how well you can do this, nor get a chance to know what you have to improve unless you try.

It may seem like hitting a home run is the safest thing to do to improve your score, but it lacks the thrill of outsmarting your opponents if you get to make it home stealing bases. The latter tests your skills, brings variety to the game, as well as creating opportunities.

Your talents and capabilities need you to tap into to sharpen your skills and knowledge of how they can best work for you. Stretch yourself to the limit to get to fulfil your potential.

Using your skills to maximum advantage makes use of your many talents and you get to do that which only you can do. You will be able to affect all areas of your life, creating a balance. This you can never achieve unless you concentrate fully and make sure that you are aware of what you do with every momemt of your time.

You do not have to grow to reach old age for your worth to be felt or recognized. Making each moment of your life count will be a guarantee to accomplishing great things even whilst young. The memories I have of my brother made me realize that he lived his life 'fast' – here one moment and gone the next. Although he died in his early thirties he was a great pilot. He seemed to be in his element when he focused on the work he enjoyed most. It was when talking to him that you would realize what it took to accomplish in that field: honed skills, sharp reflexes and admirable competencies necessary for instant decision making in an emergency. In the last days of his life he talked about what he realized was his 'unfulfilled dreams'. It was not his work that concerned him but other areas of his life. Indeed he recognized that although he had accomplished a lot in his career, he could still have done more not because his life was cut short, but that he could have done more with what he had; that was a sad moment for both of us. A point in life where if I had it in me to reverse his situation I could have done so to give him a chance to add more quality to his life.

This not just because I loved him, not because it would have been a human life saved, but, an opportunity to see the power of human talent take its rightful place.

To measure your life success you need the right yardstick. It cannot be how long you live, nor should it be based on the wealth you accumulate. Your success should be based on the worth of your donation.

Making your life count starts with making every moment count. Use your time well. Concentrate on making the best of yourself. Acquiring skills and developing competencies will provide you the tools to use on your life journey. Gained skills will be your source of wealth enabling you to accumulate whatever treasures you pursue. You sharpen and perfect skills when you manage what you have so that it continues to grow. Over time you can look back with pride when you are able effortlessly draw from your reserves of accomplishments appreciating your achievements without regretting wasted time. No matter how old you are, when you make every moment count you are on an achievement-accumulating curve. You will in time appreciate time well spent.

Remember, life is a journey you undertake starting when you are born. You are responsible for the sites and heights you reach along the way. You could choose what you think is the easy way out – the mindless, no responsibility route. However, with time the lack of focus, the feeling of wasted time, the helplessness and regrets of 'if only' will come to haunt you. You have to grow to be your true self. Only then will the satisfaction that you have done what you were supposed to will be truly yours.

Make every moment of your life count. Even when you are visiting with friends, opting for quite moment, the material you read, and many more, should all build you. It will add to making the journey positively memorable.

2

Take on the journey with Confidence

*Inform yourself so that whatever you
do you do with confidence knowing that
which you have to do and you can do.*

Confidence is about trusting more in what you can do
and when you play up what you cannot do confidence
fades away.

We get to develop confidence through our daily
experiences. You may fail at something, but if you get
to realise that it is no reflection on your abilities you
will be able to bounce right back to work on getting
it right.

Success in your past serves as the
starting point for all the other good
things that you can do.

In sports, people tend to talk about how their team has a good record track when it has to meet another team. The rival team, no matter how good it may be, will always behave like an underdog as long as record shows it usually comes out second best. The psychological advantage always persists even though the opposing team may have grown in strength since the previous encounter. The team that is the favourite to win tends to goes into the game more confident and this is half the battle won.

Your state of mind contributes a lot to your performance. When you strongly believe in that you will do well, then you will.

On preparing for a game, the coaching has to concentrate on the team's best display. It has to play up individual player's most fantastic performances. This boosts the team morale more than any form of physical training can. Often, for most players, they sub-consciously get prepared for a repeat performance or better. In the same way, it gets very difficult for a team with a history of poor performance to get over the stigma. They do not have past positive anchors to rely on. Although they may get to be physically prepared, they need a lot more to raise their spirits, building in them a mental attitude that will get them to believe more in what they can do than what they are known to have done. A positive mental state will transform the team into a winning machine.

Belief releases creative powers,
disbelief puts the brakes on.

It is when we believe that we can that we start to think constructively and our minds create ways to get us to where we want to go.

If you believe you can, often you will find that you are right, you will. A positive mental state gives you faith that whatever you may want to achieve, you will achive. You begin to work for it with confidence. Whatever position you hold at work, you will find that it is your successes that will give you the courage to keep going, continuing to persue assignments no matter how difficult. Confidence grows as you get positive feedback from your supervisor as well as the experience of satisfaction you get by doing your work successfully. It is the successes, no matter how small that will continue to feed your confidence.

Confident people get to trust their instincts and ability to cope with decisions they make. They show more originality and creativity.

As a leader, you will find that building confidence in the people you work with can yield better results than your relying on giving them rules to follow. It is only when they realise they are valued and respected that they would be willing to take risks and put to test any new ideas they have.

Confidence comes to us when we feel appreciated and needed wherever we are. Taking other people's efforts for granted kills the spirit of creativity. Creativity takes a person out of obscurity into the limelight. To be able to survive such an inconspicuous position, you will need to have it in you not to be fazed by failure and you use your successes to drive you on. You have to believe more in possibilities and creating your own opportunities.

A person with positive self-regard is
rarely, if ever, stopped by criticism or
negative sanction.

It is easy to do what other people tell you to do, as
well as doing what you are used to. Trying out what
you have never done before, or that which those around
you are not used to is risky. If a new idea or a way of
doing things does not work out, people may notice and
it may seem that you are a failure who should have
stayed with the less interesting but tested ways. You
also stand to be criticised for having changed the way
things were done. It takes a person with confidence to
objectively look at what happened and how it can best
be turned around to advantage.

We sometimes give advice to people we work or live
with. When giving advice or trying to help or build
other people's confidence, it is important to ensure
they understand where you are coming from. Until
the people you deal with are totally convinced of your
unconditional belief in what they can do, any form of
criticism, negative or so called constructive, will most

likely destroy them. More often than not, the advice, though meant to help the other person to develop, tends to be regarded as taking a shot at the personality. It is only when those you help are convinced that you genuinely care that they really listen, get to read the real intended message without taking offence.

When you believe, your mind finds a way to do. Believe that you can and you will.

If you believe you can, you will be able to do anything you put your mind to doing and look out for real builders for your life. That is the power of positive thinking.

To build self-confidence you have to take advantage of your strong points. You have to get used to doing well and learning to handle success. Success, even if it is on small things, feeds your confidence. After this, you will find it easy to try out new ideas. Having become aware of the fact that you are capable of succeeding, then any failures will be accepted and dealt with objectively.

Do everything you have to do well and let all successes, big and small, boost your confidence.

Self-confidence is about coming to respect yourself and working with your positive self to get to succeed in what you desire.

Build self-confidence

To continue your journey to the top it is your self-confidence that will keep driving you. You want to be confident and feel confident too. True self-confidence is not an overnight acquisition, nor is it something you get on someone else's 'say so'. With self-confidence you will feel unstoppable that you can do anything rather than feeling scared to do what you face. Your perception of yourself also has an enormous impact on how others perceive you – the encouragement they give you, the tasks they assign you and the tolerance of your mistakes, are all related to what they think you can do.

Take time to consciously do things that will help you to build self-confidence:

Recognize your insecurities for what they are

Take whatever makes you feel unworthy, ashamed or inferior as a warning for a silent inner voice that if allowed to persist will sabotage you, preventing you from holding your head up. Take step to work on your insecurity by talking about it to someone you trust – a parent, relative or friend. By not hiding it from yourself and others you will begin to make inroads and chip away at it. No matter how long it takes, keep working on it. Remember, you can never move on unless you resolve a situation that holds you back. Sometimes you may not be able to get rid of what holds you back. But you can make its hold on you less effective when you acknowledge its limiting power and choose to not let it do than to you any more.

Identify and make use of your strengths and successes

Find what you are good at, those things that you enjoy doing and/or excel in. These are the talents that you have to concentrate on making use of. Give yourself permission to take pride in what you do best, allow yourself to enjoy whatever successes you achieve.

Whatever you do, do not compete with the next person. This is about what you can do. By recognizing what you are good at you allow yourself to seek more ways of using your strengths more. Every success you achieve, no matter how small, will increase your self-confidence.

When you do something you enjoy, it makes you better at it, increasing your skills. It also has therapeutic effect making you feel unique, accomplished and worthy. By succeeding with a few of the things you engage in, you will find it easier to try out new and more things, as such widening your base.

Speak up and make your opinion known
Learn to speak up to make your opinion known. Making your opinion known helps you clarify your thoughts further, improves your knowledge base, increase your skills of speaking in public and relating to others, and will all generally add to your feeling of self-worth.

Keeping quiet during discussions could be a sign that you are afraid that others will judge you for saying something stupid. Indeed you could say something stupid if you have no clue what is being discussed. So, inform yourself.

Being knowledgeable and being actively aware of what you actually know and can do increase your confidence. It is only then that you are in a position to use it to advantage.

Positively contribute to the lives others
Focus more on the difference you make in the lives of others. This will make you aware how much others may be 'worse off' than you are, as such your presumed flaws will be less glaring. Your self-confidence will increase allowing you to do whatever you have to efficiently. As you contribute more towards other people's welfare, success will come easier to you and will receive more recognition from others. Then you will know you are a positive force in the world, in turn boosting your confidence.

Without confidence, the journey you take will be rocky, directionless, and you will most likely miss your target destination. When you believe that you can do and achieve something, then indeed, you will.

3

Have control over your thoughts

Being poor and being rich are the offspring of our thoughts. Whatever you think, that is what you become.

Negative thoughts are a heavy burden to carry. They lead to anxiety, greed, envy and the tendency to want to own that which you do not deserve. They lead to seemingly baseless anger, fear and being threatened by insignificant things around you. These can include a way of thinking such as believing your siblings are always sneering at you since you think they consider themselves more successful than you, to people are always against you, and they never accept what you say. You may be thinking that some things come easily to some people, they get better recognition and exposure, they make more money than you do, live in better homes, and so forth.

Negative thoughts prevent you from recognizing the real truth. You fail to recognize the hard work each of the people put in as well as characteristics they have which they may have worked hard to develop. If you always think negative, you will never benefit from your experiences; you interpret all things around negatively and keep looking for more negatives. You focus your energy on wrong things.

Emotions such as greed, fear, envy and insecurity are never subject to reason. They often fuel themselves into unfounded realities. You need to recognise them for the monsters that they are.

All negative thoughts wrap so tightly around your mind that it gets to be difficult for anything positive to creep closer.

Another source of constant negative thought is unforgiving thoughts. These keep your mind constantly fanning your anger or hatred and you actively think of ways of revenging.

Failure to forgive mainly causes damage to your soul, you get personally hurt and lose peace of mind. You spend precious time and energy plotting and counter plotting - wanting to cause others damage only to come out the loser. As John Mason puts it, 'If revenge is sweet, why does it leave a bitter taste?' You have to learn to let go of things that hurt you and release your mind to concentrate on things that are likely to build you.

A person who forgives those who injured him or her has the makings of greatness. It is those who dare forgive an injury who are strong and likely to concentrate on important issues that will bring out the best in them.

Negative thoughts can create monsters and breathe live into them. When allowed to persist such thoughts can cripple you for they bring to live that which never happened.

Thinking has a snowballing effect. As you get caught up in your thoughts, you start finding even greater detail for it, though it may not exist. You eventually become uptight and incredibly agitated. The anger and hate you allow to fester in you usually grows out of proportion and become a full time engagement. Your mind gets to be very busy nurturing the negative. It takes a lot of effort and energy to keep negative thoughts alive than positive thoughts. You need to find ways of releasing it to engage in positive thoughts.

Nothing will ever change for you until you change what goes on in your subconscious mind.

Positive thoughts of love, happiness and the desire to do good will drive you to always look for the good in all people, appreciate them and love all things. Nurturing good thoughts directs your actions to be positive. Whatever thought that runs actively in your mind you act it. Where a person thinks of succeeding in life and leaving a positive mark as opposed to drifting along, she or he thinks of ways of getting there. It is positive thinking, believing that it can be done, that will bring the desired success.

Constant exposure to a thought and related acts will lead to a habit. Over time you act without even realizing that such a thought has been going on in your mind.

Guard your mind, do not allow it to dwell on any form of negative thoughts. Guide it towards positive constructive thoughts. Equally constructive actions will inevitably follow.

As long as you allow positive thoughts
to florish, as long as you think you will
achieve your goals, you are already
ninety percent of the way there.

To get your mind to release depressing and demeaning thoughts, you have to actively think of something positive that will counter the source of the negative thoughts. Sometimes you see and marvel at great deeds by people with disabilities. They get to achieve great things which some strong bodied men and women fail to accomplish. What you have to wonder is what really drives them, why are they so successful. On the other hand, you find other people, with the same disability, feeling sorry for themselves and behaving like they are owed. Such people demand to be served, feel that other people have to pay for their disability. The difference lies with the way each person thinks. One person can look at his or her disability and decide it is a fact they cannot change, and goes ahead and takes advantage of all the other strengths they have to build a successful life. To such people success is not thought of in rigidly set dimensions, it becomes anything that brings joy into their lives. The other people consider their disability as a burden to share with all people around them. Their anger at having been singled out for it only makes them bitter and angry. They thus have no time for anything else.

We all are capable of negative thinking, but we need the strength to cultivate positive thoughts. You have to become a master at directing your straying thoughts.

If you think good about yourself you will get to think the same about others. Whatever you think of others will be reflected in the way you treat them and react when in their presence. As such you will strive to get the best out of everyone. An act is achievable if you have your thoughts focused on doing great things for all.

It is impossible to hold down anyone without staying down with them. For the person to stay where you want them to be, you have to keep them company. Should you think negative of others, such thoughts could only drag you down to where you want those others to be. Your actions will be geared towards your thoughts and in the end you become what you think.
You cannot say it nor act it unless you have thought about it.

A thought is a most potent form of suggestion - often more powerful than any received through the sense of sight, hearing, smell, taste and touch. Your subconscious mind has known and unknown powers, and you must control them to win over yourself. - W. Clement Stone

When we think of a person going through life happily it is never as one governed by negative thoughts where bitterness and anger would reign for instance. Good life is about happiness and joy. These, for different people come from different sources. No one is ever happy when they cannot find their worth and can clearly show and see that they are good for something. Those who depend on others for every thing get to feel the need to find something they can do that they can call their own.

Find your purpose. Think about what you want and let your thoughts drive you on. Let your thoughts be the dream that guides you finding yourself.

4

Become a total winner

Talents are common, everyone has them. But only a few people have the courage to follow their talents where they lead.

To succeed in life, you have to first win the battle from within you. It is your view of life that determines what happens to you. What happens in you is the active thoughts going on in your mind; these will influence your actions, and eventually become what you act.

You cannot accept the norm as a standard and expect to rise to do great things. It is those who challenge tradition who make history.

Win yourself over by thinking positive. Get to be positive about yourself, act positive and your view of life will in turn change to be positive. You will begin to see good in all thing around you and in other people. Your actions will compliment your outlook. To be anything else means being uncomfortable and suspicious with other people's motives and paranoid about what happens to you. Jan Christiaan Smuts once said, "A man is not defeated by his opponents but by himself." To win in what you want to do, it is wise to conquer yourself first before you take on the world.

There are usually more who say, "you can't" than those who say "I can". And it is the latter who transform dreams into reality.

Consider how you will feel if I was to offer you a glass that is half filled with water. Do you consider the glass to be half empty or is it half full? If it is half full, you will receive it with sincere gratitude; where you think it is half empty it will be received accompanied by some negative thoughts. Yet, the glass contains exactly the same amount of water, no matter which way you look at it. It is all in the attitude. A positive attitude will make you look at events from the good they can bring or the good they represent whilst negative attitude makes you dredge up what any action failed to cater for. A positive outlook will make you expect the best of everything, not the worst; you will see posibilities and solutions in every problem and not problems in all solutions that are available to you. You will remain optimistic that the best is still to come even when others say it is hopeless.

It is easy to believe your doubts and to doubt your beliefs. Strengthen your faith in your beliefs, all doubts will lose their significance.

To win the battle against failing, you do not just need to be positive, you have to enjoy the satisfaction that comes with success. That feeling of contentment may at times be the only reward you will get for what you do.

As your outlook improves you get to believe more in what you can do and tend to see good in others rather than the shortcomings. You are not fazed by problems you face, you tend to deal with adversity in a way that turns it to advantage. Failures experienced are temporary setbacks you overcome as you steadily take steps towards your goal.

Do not allow momentary setbacks to become the tombstone of your career. Turn setbacks into stepping stones to greater achievements.

Make use of all resources available to you, especially other people. You cultivate a people first attitude, and this caring attitude makes it easy for people to want to work with you and have them work for you. You learn from others and will easily turn what you learn to greater advantage.

A person wrapped up in himself or herself
makes a pretty small package.

Trying to do all things on your own will only make you do less and achieve less. To work with others gives strength and you achieve more quickly that otherwise will take long to come to you.

Your dream will not come true if you are sleeping - you have to work your dream. If you wait for others to give you what you want without working for it you will only get what they can spare.

The important thing is not what happens to you but what happens inside you. Failure is as much an inside job as is success. In both cases you are the only person who decides for you what it is going to be. Real limitations or winners are created in the mind. It is your attitude that will determine how you respond to what happens to you.

5

Motivation gives you momentum

It is those who are weak who wait for opportunities; those who are strong make their opportunities.

Top success is reserved for the I-can-do-it better kind of person. Great success calls for people who continually set high standards for themselves and others, people who are searching for ways to increase efficiency, to get more output at lower cost - do more for less effort

---

Motivation can fade but habit prevails.

You cannot achieve anything of significance if you are not driven to make it your own. To get to do it, you talk yourself into it and act on it. Once you are used to doing, it is a habit that will always be there for you. It keeps you going even if what first started you off may lose its attraction.

Successful people take initiative, engage in purposeful actions, show a strong desire to get to the top, are persistent and very intense in showing a singleness of mind. Such people are definitely motivated. If you give up before you get anything done, then you will fail. Sometimes you may feel you have the best reasons and explanations why you couldn't do it. But, the bottomline remains, 'you have not done it'. Take advantage of the drive you feel within, the belief that you must do something, and stand up and act.

Hope keeps us striving for a better future; without it we give up in despair.

Motivation is influenced by beliefs, attitudes and emotions. If you strongly believe you have to do something, it is that desire that will drive you forth. Set up all things that will contribute to your success to get you there.

Motivation provides a deep desire to achieve - the motive. A motive is the drive from within you, the "inner urge" which incites you to action. It comes in the form of an idea, an emotion, a desire, or an impulse. Motivation influences initiative, direction, intensity of action and persistence of behaviour.

If I had not been motivated to write this book I would have stopped before it was completed. The urge to write was a result of the deep emotion I experienced because of the tragedy of losing someone I loved. The grief I went through could have consumed my energy to the point where I could lose focus. It was the hope I had that some day things will become better that made it possible to go on. By putting my thoughts on paper I got motivated by the knowledge that one day someone will benefit from these words.

What is it that motives you? Find a way of packaging it. Remember that only you can do it your way. It could be something you do just for the joy of creating something new. It could be what you need to solve a major problem in your life. Whatever it is, stand up and do it. Once your mind focuses on what you do you will have the momentum you need to see your project through.

A motivated person sets goals and works out how to achieve these. Goals set are influenced by 'ability' and general feelings of self-worth. These will influence how much effort a person expends on attaining the set goals. The inner urge of your feelings, emotions, instincts and ingrained habits will give you the go-power that puts you into action.

Dissatisfaction with what is, sets the mind working to seek ways to act, looking for solutions. It is only when you have realised that your life has fallen into a rut that you can hope to reach out and work on improving you situation. This gives you inspiration to action, the motivation you need to start going.

If you keep thinking ahead, thinking always of trying to do more, giving your best, it will bring you a state of mind in which nothing is impossible. This is the confidence you need to keep moving forward.

Motivated People:

> live with the question 'how can I improve the quality of my performance?'

> are willing to take risks, believe in what they can do and achieve;

> maintain unflagging optimism that their effort will pay off;

> are focused on long term success rather than short term;

> use expressions such as 'I did it before, I can do it again';

> Set goals high and workout a strategy to achieve them;

> look upon failure as a temporary setback;

> regard failure as a challenge and strive to overcome it;

> use present failure as an experience from which to workout future action;

> use mapped out strategy to monitor performance;

> instruct themselves to exert greater effort;

> enjoy and relish challenge.

It is only when you are motivated that you see opportunities around you instead of problems. You find ways of always doing your best.

> *The power to create quality life is not in any planner. It is not in any technique or tool. And it is not limited to our ability to plan a day. . .*
> *. . . The power to create quality of life is within us - in our ability to develop and use our own inner compass so that we can act with integrity in the moment of choice.   - Covey & Merrill*

Be happy that you still get a chance daily to do something about your life. Let the fact that you are in a position to do something be motivation enough to keep moving forward. Keep at it until the habit of doing drives you incessantly.

6

Your attitude as a key to success

*Every garden reflects how it is looked after,
the actions taken to control weeds and pests.
These affect the final product.*

Take charge of your destiny
Life is really what you make of it – make your life
count. No one can make your dreams come true for
you except yourself. So, believe that you are in charge
of your destiny and do all you can to make it a reality.
Remember that, by doing nothing for your life you are
creating your life – and you may not like the product. A
positive attitude will enable you to be actively involved
in creating a life you want, which you can enjoy.

No one is ever proud of second-rate product. You too need a positive attitude that will make you truly successful living a life you enjoy. Start by learning to have a positive attitude. As you go through life and face challenges you will be able to optimistically keep going allowing you a chance to get to know what you can truly become.

You are the sum total of the choices you make and actions you carry out daily.

Attitudes are mirrors of the mind, they reflect our thinking. Our thoughts become our words, words which lead to actions that we take. Actions repeated over time become a habit. Habits get to be associated with you, they become your character. Character matures into a personality, the stuff that ordains our destiny.

Attitude is read through facial expressions, voice tones and inflections, the quality of your smile and the amount of enthusiasm displayed in all you do.

Liven up everything you do: your hand shake, your talk, your thank you - say it with life. Your enthusiasm will soon catch all people around you - enthusiasm is contagious. People cannot help it but join you in displaying enthusiasm and acting like you.

When our attitude is right our abilities reach maximum effectiveness and good results inevitably follow. Grow the attitude of 'I'm activated' and positively influence those around you.

As you deal with others treat them as important and be prepared to provide first rate service at all times. All people want to feel important, and they will do more for you when you make them important not because they think you are important. Successful people work on having 'small' people feeling big and 'big' people feeling even bigger. The end result is everyone feels bigger than before and behave in a way that is consistent with how they feel.

Find good in all people, and work on creating opportunities for them to do their best. Give compliments and always show your appreciation of others. This will boost their confidence in a big way and will make them work better and for more.

Strive to always leave others better than you found them. Sometimes, just a smile will do. For some, a word of comfort, of goodwill, or just showing recognition will be required. Actively interact with others, do not just drift by.

Praise the people you work with. Learn to share with them your own successes. Be prepared to take a little more than your share of the blame and take a little less than your share of the credit. Others will be encouraged to do even more for you.

Out of the gloom a voice said unto me "smile and be happy, things could be worse!" So I smiled and was happy and indeed, things did get better. - Peter Ellis

---

Attitude always makes a difference. It makes things happen, for better – for worse. Whether you think you can or you can't, you will usually be right. It is the state of your mind that drives you to find a way or not to. As long as you think you can, then you will find a way to do just that. Of course if you believe you cannot, then you are unlikely to make any effort to get to do it - 'where there is a will, there is a way'. The way you think and react when you lose determines how long it will be until you start winning again.

The True riches of life are hidden in the
hearts and minds of all men and women.
All we need to do is create the right
climate for these to flourish.

In your attitude, you may believe that failing to get what you wanted is a sign that you are a failure, or you may choose to look at it as a learning opportunity, allowing you to try again as a better informed person.

Every setback you go through represents a learning experience. Have the courage to reconstruct your situation so that you know why you failed. In future, you will do things differently.

Use challenges faced as boosters for increased perfomance. Accept that there is no success without sweat. Create a success habit and be prepared to live up to your own expectations. Be aware that your greatest achievement today is only a mediocre performance tomorrow. Use your experiences of today to accomplish bigger and better in the future. In the process you will be proud of the person you become.

> Great achievers never reach the end of
> success. They always set higher standards,
> bigger goals, and improve on what is.
> They are always willing to find out what is
> it that is out of sight.

Work on becoming the person you would be proud
to be. It is only your attitude that will make all the
difference in the end.

If you seek the essence of perfection
*   You become perfect*
If you seek the essence of success
*   You become more successful*
If you seek the essence of achievement
*   You achieve more*
If you seek the essence of anything
*   you strive for specific major objectives, with*
*   singleness of purpose*
With each step forward you get closer and closer
*   to the essence you seek.*
(Adapted from The success System that never fails
by W. Clement Stone)

7

The giving attitude

It is not more strength, nor more ability,
neither is it great opportunity that we need.
We just need to use what we have.

Giving the best at all times is a sure way to enjoy living one's life. You get personally fulfilled as you see your effort come to fruition. To get to give your best involves making choices as you face the many alternative ways of doing things. Every time you successfully solve a problem, it gives satisfaction. Human beings are meant to live on meaningful gains - that which one has personally done. The better you do, the greater the satisfaction.

The act of making a decision and seeing how your decision works out is the reward that brings you satisfaction. Doing your best in every thing enables you to discover even more opportunities for your talents and abilities to be put into practice.

When the best of you at any given time has been revealed, you will find a need to test and stretch it even further. You become a possibility thinker. The activity knowledge that comes to you through experience, gets to be tested in new ways allowing your creative self to keep coming with even better, bigger and more interesting achievements. Once you have experienced the feel of success, you believe less in things being impossible, and to you, whatever your mind can think of has to be made to work.

A person who always thinks about what needs to be done, in the best way possible, gets the best out of everything and everyone. If you get the best out of everyone, it is in itself a sign that you have leadership skills without which people will never trust you enough to take your advice. You can never succeed until all others around you successfully work towards the set goals with you. Get them to succeed and your success will inevitably follow.

You will not succeed unless you are willing to make decisions about what is to be done and commit to seeing it done. You have to keep making more and more decisions no matter how many mistakes you make in the process. Without making decisions, no new ideas will be tried out - things around you will remain the same as always. You need to make your own decisions rather than do that which others think is good for you.

All things around us were once just ideas. The developments we see around us today represent decisions taken to transform those ideas into reality.

The one thing that remains constant on the way to success seems to be making mistakes, from which you have to recover and move on. Making small decisons can only lead to making few mistakes and inevitably small successes. If you only make small decisions, so will your rate of growth and success be small and if

you are able to overcome big obstacles you will grow
by the same magnitude. Making big decisions lead
to great successes, though may often be checkered by
big failure enroute.

If you only make small decisions, so will
be your rate of growth and success.

As you get used to making decisions, your ability
to analyse a situation and arrive at a reasonable
conclusion gets to be good and you are able to make
such decisions quickly. The decisions you make get to
be accurate most of the time. Successes you enjoy as
you decide on issues lead to an increase in self-esteem
and you will become more assertive. It it those who
make decisions and act on them who progress. They
are become aware what does not work and will have
a chance to use what works best.

Learn from your mistakes and gain the experience
you will need as you make decisions in the future.
Expect obstacles and be prepared to face them
rather than avoid them. Challenge provides you an
opportunity to develop your talent. Every time you face
a major difficulty it is like reaching a road junction. You

choose which route you will follow. It could be toward
breakdown or breakthrough. Challenges are transient.
They come and go. When you allow temporary setback
to defeat you, then you fail. You can use setbacks to
teach you how to do things better than you did before.
Then you will get closer to achieving greater things.

The mistake-riddled life is much richer,
more interesting, and more stimulating
than life that has never risked or taken a
stand on anything. It is the uncertainty of
it that keeps the curiosity and motivation
high.

Learn from your mistakes, use your experience to
keep moving forward. Keep doing, until you get things
right. Do not give up. Settling for anything else is a
recipe for mediocrity and failure. Your potential will
remain unfulfilled, denying you a chance to experience
what might have been.

A mistake made is an opportunity to work out
why things did not work; use it as a starting point for
an alternative line of action. Besides, you now know

what does not work.

Your success is measured by how much of what you are supposed to do you do well. Do all that you have to do well. It will make you happy and develop the liking for success.

People's self-worth tends to increase as they enjoy success in what they do. Self-satisfaction makes you respect yourself, builds your confidence and you believe even more in what you can do. This feeling of confidence grows even further when other people recognise your worth based on how successful you are. But it is what you belief about yourself that has the greatest impact.

Success comes to those who believe in their own ability to change, who can work out a plan to get to where they want to go, and who can act on their plan to achieve through excellence.

People usually respect you when they recognise in you that you care for them. Caring comes in the form of helping them experience success in their own right.

You love and respect yourself more when you do good; succeeding at what you do, being appreciated for the thing you do and can do. Believing in what you can do leads to you striving for more. It even gets easier to inspire others to do like you.

Whatever you do that contributes to your growth is an investment that you can draw from in the future. The more you do, the better you become.

People who give their best are those who serve well. It has many rewards.

- skill acquired work for you as you become a good problem solver
- you achieve the highest possible level for you and do not settle for mediocre performance
- your capacity to learn increases proportionally
- you use your newly acquired skills to generate new ideas and come up with new ways of working.

In order to bring the best out of yourself, you need to put in the right ingredients which when they blend will give a respectable product. Be prepared to work, accept that you will make mistakes as you try out your ideas. Expect obstacles which when you overcome, you gain the experience that will give the unique you. Your talents and abilities will remain hidden if you do not make the effort to uncover them.

Only you can do what has to be done for you to achieve the success you desire. In doing all that you have to do you become skilled and knowledgeable – developing capabilities that you need to achieve your life's successes. Everything that you learn becomes part of your life's investment. It is this that you draw from every time you carry out a task. You will be worth what you keep depositing into your account. The more you deposit the more resourceful you will be. By allowing yourself to be a doer, a giver, serving others diligently you set yourself up for a satisfying life. You acquire skills and knowledge you need to competently fulfill your dreams.

You cannot hope to solve big problems before you solve your basic problem - victory over yourself. You are your worst enemy. The one you have to conquer and discipline first.

8

Today's thoughts are tomorrow's reality

No one can change yesterday. What happened then is a reality that today starts off from. Today is still here for you, live it well for tomorrow will look back to it for a head start.

"There are three things that can never be retrieved - the spoken word, time past and neglected opportunity." (old muslim saying). Allowing time to go by without utilizing it profitably means you lose the chance to meet your obligations, that is opportunity past.

You may brag all you want about what you will do tomorrow, the fact is that it may never get done. The day you had in mind might dawn only to seem like yet another busy day leaving you hoping there will be a better tomorrow. Do what you have to do now, do it today, do not wait for tomorrow.

> Tomorrow is often the busiest day of
> the week. - Spanish Proverb

Indecision is a time waster. It allows you to postpone what you can do now to another time, only to find that it gets to be even more difficult to do then. The best thing to do is to do what has to be done when it is to be done. That will leave the future for more things to do. A job not done when it is to be done is a burden on the mind. It keeps nagging throughout the day even as you do other things.

> If you do that which is to be done
> today well, you know that you have
> prepared well for tomorrow.

Tomorrow is already full as it is. You have a lot to do in that day without adding today's chores to it. Those who push things to tomorrow are those who are not intending to grow; those who do not achieve anything great. They do the minimum they can possibly get away with in any day.

Do what you have to do when it is to be done. It is only then that, when you reflect on all the time you had you will notice it is time well spent.

We can leave tomorrow for the lazy person, who will of course soon realize that yesterday's work is even more difficult to do today than it was before. Tomorrow is the only day in the week that appeals to a lazy person. This being the difference between those people who never make it and those who do.

People with 'no work' or little work to do often seem to have no time to do anything. They are busy waiting to do nothing. In the end they get irritated and depressed when they think about time. They know they have to account for their time, even to themselves, yet there is nothing new forthcoming. As such when what you are to do is decided and is done earlier, you are left with nothing to decide. Time demands the responsibility of deciding how to spend it.

Successful people seem to be ever so busy, and yet

take on even more reponsibility, only to fulfil their promises when those with less to do can only come back to offer excuses for the little they should have done. Those watching tend to ask : 'where do they get the time?' 'Do they ever rest?' and so forth. Yes, do they have more hours and minutes in a day than you do? Definitely not. What is it about these people that makes it possible for them to stretch the day? They are not only driven, but they are focused and have no intention of getting where they want to go by chance. Through doing they gain skills. They do what they have to do quickly - efficiently and effectively. They have learnt to multiply themselves through enlisting the assistance of others. They will not be satisfied with anything less than their desired goal.

Indecision is a time waster. It allows you to postpone what you can do now to another time. Act on your decisions promptly. The best time is now. If you wait, all the small and easy things will accumulate and become hard work. They become your future emergencies. They become the reason you work overtime. Anything that you failed to do yesterday gets to be difficult to do today, and it will be even more difficult tomorrow.

Time cannot be controlled, you can only control yourself. Discipline yourself to do what you have to do when you have to do it. As the saying goes, "time waits for no man."

Great things come from all the little things that we do. It is important that we keep doing all things because if they are the foundation of great things then they are not little after all.

To be successful you have to plan your time. You will get the benefit of each moment to get you to where you want to go.

When you do not plan your time, you get to do anything that drifts your way, including the unimportant. You are able to postpone some of your work to another day since you are unable to see beyond now.

Learn to manage your time to get to use it profitably. Time management is about setting clear priorities for yourself and making sure you achieve them; it is about recognising that time is a wasting resource: when it is gone it is gone, you never get it back. Have a purpose and set clear goals of where you want to go. Decide on the steps you will take to get there. Allocate a time when each of your goals will be achieved. Discipline yourself to stick to your plan. It is you that you have to control, not time.

Time is constant, you have the same number of seconds in a minute, and same number of hours in a day as everyone. You can only change what you do, how you do it, in the available time.

As you act promptly on all matters you lay the foundation for the future. Whatever you are able to do or you have is a product of the past. Things are the way they are because you acted as you did.

Plan your time, then you will be able to :
- use it more effectively
- do more in the available time
- feel more relaxed and in control of your time
- have time for work and time for yourself and your family

Whatever you do or use, someone has to pay for it. As someone spends time assisting you there is a cost to it. 'Time is money' – indeed the person could be earning elsewhere. Use your time profitably at all times. Even as you sit relaxing with others, keep your mind learning – use the opportunity to learn from the moment. Develop the habit of using your free time productively, you will feel better fulfilled as a result. Have something concrete planned that you do and you have to show results for doing. This will teach you to engage in profitable deeds that can help build you.

Now, is the magic word of success. Tomorrow, next week, sometime, someday, often as not are synonyms for the failure word 'never'. Lots of good dreams never come true because we say, "I'll start some day" when we should say. "I'll start now, right now".   David J. Schwartz

The results of whatever you think of, that which you have to do today will be visible tomorrow. You are where you are today because of what you did or did not do in the past.

9

Commit and work

If you do not work it, it would never happen. Wishful thinking will not turn your desires into reality, but acting definitely will. All ideas you have will remain that until you work on them.

Without work, nothing you want will ever be realized. To get anything done requires having targets you want to meet, you put activities in place which will bring your desires to pass.

Most of the things we desire may be difficult to achieve and may have never been done before. Because they are unknown, we may find it difficult to work on them. The best thing to do to overcome the fear of doing is to stand up and do what it takes. Action drives away fear.

Any time you try to do something and
fail, you are vastly better off than if you
choose to try to do nothing and succeed.
By doing and failing you have achieved
something - knowhow, or is it how not to?

There is no success without work. To develop your latent talent to its maximum potential, you have to work. Work is the key to unlocking hidden traits which, if never tested under work pressure will not come to the fore. Work pressure makes it possible to get to know what you can really do when it comes to the crunch.

Without work we can never discover
and make use of our many talents,
skills, abilities and capabilities.

Always do the maximum possible for you, it will increase your capacity to work. In the future you will be able to handle more work at a time and even do it faster. Avoiding work does not only deny you the chance to develop your potential and gain new skills, it eventually leads to your doing even less over time. You may have noticed that people who do less work often claim to be busy, even busier than those who do more than they do. They also tend to be tired most of the time. Inactivity gets to be a pre-occupation. It leaves those who engage in it very tired.

Avoid seeking a lighter load. Doing
maximum possible in each day will
increase your capacity to work; a light
load will have you do even less over time.

Do whatever you intend to do with enthusiasm and energy. Enthusiasm will attract others to your way of thinking and doing and this can only assist you to achieve your goals.Being enthusiastic shows that you love and enjoy what you do. That can only help you find more ways of doing better. Working like that will increase your chances of succeeding, and this will increase your motivation.Actively working makes you more daring and increases your ability to innovate.

In the end you will find that the more you do, the

more you succeed, the more you seem to be capable of doing.

Capacity to perform increases as you constantly do work.

Are you in your present employment because that is what was on the offer when you desparately needed to be employed? Whatever attracted you to this job may finally lose its enticing power - you need to look for something that will interest you for longer. What are you getting out of the job more than the subsistence benefit? A job may offer you better opportunity for advancement than highest pay, or better gain in the long term than the short term. It may offer opportunity to learn and gain experience which may be more usuful to you when you need to face new and more challenging areas in the future. But, do you have anything to contribute to your job that you can uniquely call your own? Personal contribution is more likely to bring personal fulfilment more than immediate monetary gain.

> Working hard is not a substitute for strategy. Filling time is not the same as working. Attending to urgent issues is not the same as dealing with the important.

Develop the ability to stay focussed on what you want done and doing it through willing yourself to act. Do not rely on inner inspiration to be the sole source of drive to get to do work. Will your self to act, keeping at it and after ten minutes you should feel interested enough and stay with the job. Robert McKain points out, 'the common conception is that motivation leads to action, but the reverse is true - action precedes motivation'. Work starts as a conscious act intended to help us achieve desired goals. Let work be your closest friend, after all you need this friend at all times to reach success levels you dream of.

10

Develop a win-win attitude

There is no gift that lasts more than the caring attitude. People in general need care one way or the other, as a result we all care. Caring is not just smiling at the other person, it is about feelings and actions that are interpreted as caring by the recipient. It is also getting the other person to genuinely smile back.

Through your actions, make the people you serve realise you care, make each of them feel special. On providing a service, you are aiming at serving your customers' needs. In the process, customers will be delighted if you provide a little more than expected. It is this that will make them seek your service again in the future. Give your customers time and quality attention, listening and responding to whatever they have to say. On going the extra mile you give the silent message that you care, not only just selling a service but also will to share the best of yourself.

People will be willing to come back to be with you because of the satisfaction you bring them. This is a win-win situation as you too get what you want. With win-win you must give up the 'I want more than you' attitude and work toward group success.

If things are not going well with you or your business, begin your effort at correcting the situation by carefully examining the service you are rendering and especially the spirit in which you are rendering it.

Make people feel welcome and needed. When they feel special and not just one of the many they will look back to you with equal respect. Always remember to use a client's name when the chance to do so arises. It is a sign that you recognize who they are and that they matter to you; you understand and respect them as individuals. Be courteous, polite and welcoming at all times. Be good to those you work with or work for. It makes you a winner too. By presenting them in a positive light it improves working relations as well as encourage all to work with you.

Business is like a game of tennis. It is those who serve well that get to win in it.

First impressions determine whether the other person is impressed enough to come back or not. You may never get another chance in the future to correct the damage. Be welcoming, courteous and open to receive the other person unconditionally.

First impresssions are made daily with all people, including those you work and live with. The enthusiasm and genuineness behind greetings when you meet members of your family, your colleagues and clients daily, how you react at meetings and the way you deal with people over the telephone - they all matter.

In the presence of a prospective client you have to communicate interest, concern, enthusiasm and the willingness to go the extra mile.

Have something positive and genuine to say to your clients as you serve them and when you part with them. Your last word will determine whether they will come back or not. Make the people you serve feel special. Say something to or do something positive for your customer; put a smile on their faces. By so doing you will be providing a little more than is expected. By recognizing something special in your client they go away with a feeling of delight that they would be happy to repeat.

Be genuine with your client, people always know when you are a phony.

Avoid standard phrases or routine activity when you deal with your clients. Work out what each needs and respond to this. Some clients need to be chatted to whilst others may consider it a waste of their time; some need to be left alone and they will talk to you when they are ready, whilst others need to be approached and talked to; some need to be directed to get to a decision, whilst others already know what they want and would prefer to do the suggesting themselves.

It is not what you want nor what you know that

matters but what those that you serve perceive as appropriate.

The people you serve judge you on what they see, your behaviour, your attitude and what they get out of it, never on your intentions. As Henry Ford once said, 'You can't build a reputation on what you're going to do.' Provide good service first, your reputation will be made.

Show enthusiasm as you serve all people. Be excited about all clients. Even those making small orders, they are likely to grow with you, when the big businesses may have already reached capacity or only have small potential for further expansion. There is more to make from small, reliable, repeat business. It is always available for you.

Whatever you do to make your customer happy it comes back to you in all the relationships you set up.

Shoddy work is a sign of disrespect to
both the self and to the people you serve.

We communicate to people by way of what we do or fail to do, the things we actually say or fail to say. It matters therefore that you communicate clear intended messages.

Check your people skill and make sure you know what your client needs. It is what you know about your business, your skills and your attitude towards your client that will make or break your business.

People do judge the book by the cover. The tone and lay-out of your correspondence, the quality of brochure and marketing material, the appearance of staff the customers meet, the condition and appearance of company transport, the physical environment into which the customer comes - how does it look, sound, smell, and what are the messages it carries about the company's attitude to the customer? If you are to remain competitive, you have to put things right - serve to please. Make everybody feel welcome, appreciative. They will enjoy the moment, the environment and look forward to the service. They win, you win.

Giving excellent performance is not about being101 percent better at one thing but being 1 percent better at a 100 things; - learn to do well at more than one thing.

You are in business as long as there are people willing to be served by you. Set the stage right, they will always be there for you.

Win-win attitude is a mental habit. Like all habits it takes time to acquire and you have to consciously work at it. Start slow and work your way up. As you experience the good feelings with each win-win situation in your life, it will become easier to adapt your thinking and actions for the next opportunity. The confidence that comes with 'effectively closing' each win-win situation will enhance the way to look at life every time. You will consciously begin to experience gaining wisdom where you even realize that loving and caring for others is the investment for successful living we all need – the ultimate win-win situation.

11

Discipline leads to great achievements

All people need to take control of their lives to make sure it takes the direction that they like. It takes a disciplined mind and strength of character to ensure self-control that keeps one's life on the desired route.

Self-control keeps you going when you know that you could be else-where having an easier time than what you have to do. With discipline, you are better able to overcome anything that stops you from doing what you have to do. Discipline begins with small things done daily. With a well disciplined mind you create your own luck, you overcome obstacles that will always face you on your way to achieving your goals. You learn to be patient and persevere to get to where you want to go. You grow to realize that there is no success without work.

> To be disciplined is to go for what
> you want without giving in when
> things go tough.

The secret behind most success stories is discipline, having what it takes to stay on, knowing when to change direction, when to press harder and when to give in when there is no other way forward. All people who are worth their salt appreciate the grind, the discipline they have to exercise to get where they want to be. When you give up before you arrive, it shows that you are not disciplined enough, you do not have what it takes to go the distance. You have to win the victory over yourself to be confident that you will always do what you have to, set great goals knowing you have the staying power to see them through. Discipline is about learning new and better ways of doing things and coping with situations on your way to achieving desired results.

Self-discipline should come first if you are to achieve success. Most of us do dream of great achievement one day. But we tend to settle for the next best thing as we find that getting to where we want to go is not easy. Discipline involves learning when you are to do things that have to be done, even if it means delaying or giving up other things to wait for what you want. Settling for instant gratification means you grab at a moments pleasure, when you could have had more and intense rewards by working a little longer, doing what it takes and waiting for better results. You learn to control your basic impulses, in the process developing strength of character.

To get to the top of the mountain, your set target, you have to realize that the mountain cannot make itself smaller to make it easier for you. Nor are you supposed to dream less to be said to have succeeded. Conquer yourself - your hopes, your dreams. Be selfless in striving to reach your set goal. Keep your target in mind and go for it no matter the challenges you face.

Discipline is always remembering what you want, and not allowing yourself to be side-tracked from it by transients. You choose your own laws for living and must live with the consequences of your choices. You become more accountable, taking responsibility for your decisions. Discipline is the ability to do what you should do without being distracted by a promise of easier work, or quick money as you already know what it takes to get to where you want to go.

Some people regard discipline as a chore. For me, it is a kind of necessary order that sets me free to fly. Without it I will not complete any task, especially if it becomes boring and difficult.

Self-doubt often stops us from pursuing our goals. It can come in the form of losing interest in the goals that started you off because you convince yourself that it may not be a good idea after all. As you doubt your ability to successfully carry out the task, you let your mind tune out and wonder off to other things. Thus you talk or think yourself into believing that you have out grown your original ideas. You easily take your eyes off your intended target, your focus go off the activities that should get you closer to your goals; thus you develop interest in activities that do not contribute to what you had initially intended to achieve.

In all this, you may feel temporarily fulfilled, yet in the long term you realise the dissatisfaction that comes with unfulfilled dreams. Compromising one's vision only creates a void that will forever call for fulfilment. You need to be strong enough not to give in to distractions.

After deciding on what your life would be, take responsibility for it without expecting others to be telling you what to do, how and when to do it. Or even to decide for you whether you have arrived or not. With this, you are able not to allow small successes, often inevitable on the way to big success, to make you believe that is all you deserve. Thus giving up too soon. Never stop scratching for more and better.

Discipline does not presume the right to act without regard to the effect personal decisions will have on others. You are not just concerned with what you want, you also work out how it will affect yourself and others, both in the short and long term. A truly disciplined person protects and acts responsibly on behalf of others. You learn to work with others towards the set goal.

Without discipline we will all take and do what we want when we want, with no regard for consequences to others and the future.

We need discipline if we are to achieve what we want. It is discipline that ensures that you do what has to be done when it is to be done. It is discipline that guides you to always do the right thing. The journey is long, difficult and may even be lonely. It takes discipline to stay on.

12

Integrity

We all like to be trusted and respected by others. It gives a sense of belonging and often leads one to wanting to do more just to continue to get more of the same. By feeling on the same page with your inner self, it makes you more complete, and this is an example of being regarded as having integrity.

Integrity brings about a sense of being one with self, an inner sense of 'wholeness, that strongly derives from consistency of character. Integrity is an attribute that when you have it you show positive qualities that include honesty, which in turn leads being considered reliable and can be trusted by others.

People of integrity are at one in all things they say or do. The words they say and the things that they do always match. To achieve personal effectiveness, your words must match your deeds at all times no matter where you are. Then all people who come into contact with you will understand you and know how to deal with you.They will know who you really are. Cavett Roberts sums it up well by saying, "If my people understand me, I'll get their attention. If my people trust me, I'll get their action". Integrity inspires trust. Others know what to expect from you.

Duplicity or merely pretending creates mistrust as others get to notice and they lose faith in what you do. People with no integrity find it easy to renege on promises. They take from others even what does not belong to them. When you make a promise, others are never sure whether you are telling the truth or not. They are certain that you will deliver on your promises. For that reason, people tend to prefer not to work with you. You must earn people's confidence, if they are to voluntarily work with you. Act your talk and others will do likewise.

People of integrity have nothing to hide and nothing to fear as they live what they preach. They are honest to themselves and all people around.

In order to keep promises, you have to plan your time and keep to your plan. Where you find yourself manipulating your plans, you are moving towards making excuses for not doing what you were supposed to do when it was to be done. In the end you will find that this practice is very costly. You are going to lose credibility. A person without decision of character can never be said to belong to himself. He belongs to whatever can make captive of him. Once lost, credibility will be difficult to repair, you are unlikely to find it easy to win back the trust of the people you let down, be it your colleagues or family. Children observe their parents and see how they uphold their set values. Where these are compromised, parents lose their children's trust. Sometimes, forever. Trust develops as the other person exhibits honesty consistently, over time.

When you practice honesty people are more likely to believe you and be better convinced in what you stand for than the profession of holiness.

Integrity demands inner strength - the ability to make decisions and being prepared to take responsibility for the outcomes. If you fail to meet your target you go right ahead to make up without making excuses. Excuses are rarely believed anyway. The world will not remember you for the promises you made, but for the promises you keep.

When you put the interest of the people who depend on you first, they develop trust in what you can do for them and they will in turn do the same for you. You gain loyalty and true friendship by being trustworthy. Think about what you do for people, what it means to them and your character will take care of itself. It is for this reason that you can never ask for integrity in others, unless you are blameless yourself.

People of integrity expect to be believed. They also know time will prove them right and are willing to wait and not take dubious shortcuts.

People of integrity make great leaders. They have learnt to walk their talk, as such lead by example. They value the respect of others based on what they do, as

such always seek to do the right thing at all times.
They never expect from others what they can never
themselves give.

Trust is not a gift nor a talent, but a
product of time tested character forged in
the midst of life's trials. A time-tested life
is the raw material of character and trust.
Trust must be earned. - Myles Munroe

If you understand yourself, you are better able to make
decisions that do not change with external conditions.
You make promises, be they to yourself or to others,
fully knowing what you are capable of delivering.
Knowing your weaknesses and strengths, learning to
work on your weaknesses and capitalising on your
strengths is the beginning of understanding yourself.
If you do, you will always be true to yourself.

13

Pressure Makes Diamond

The hardest substance nature ever produced, diamond, is a product of very high pressures and temperatures. What could have been ordinary lumps of coal became precious mineral of high value. Human life benefits from similar experiences. When you face difficult times you have to make decision to benefit from them by abstracting lessons the moment holds for you. Every moment of your life is full of lessons – some basic, simple and easy to follow but others you learn from defeat, disappointments and failures you suffer daily. No one has ever made it to the top without facing stern challenges. Problems solved provide the solver first hand knowledge of the realities of life. Without that experience, you might go through life believing that things are easy to get, forgetting that if they were that easy other people would grab them for themselves.

When you fail at something, it is an opportunity to start over again, better informed and more efficient to produce quality result. It is when you solve big problems that your successes get big. As you deal in small decisions, you make only small mistakes, you fail to solve big problems, as such you make only small successes.

By learning to correct small faults, you will grow to control great ones in the future.

Where people drift through success, they become complacent and fail to take time to think about how they can best serve others. Their easy success, though small, makes them believe people will always accept whatever they offer.

Most of the successes we see today are there because there was failure that preceded them. Someone at sometime past made a decision to create something new; took time to perfect it and provide the world with a useful product. Without that, we would have done things the same old ways they were done by others before us.

Failure helps us to seek alternatives that will

provide a better answer to the present and prepares us for the future.

At the top of the success ladder, you find people who once faced big obstacles and were able to overcome them. Right now, they give a picture of serenity, as if nothing ever bothers them. The confidence they show is a result of having passed the toughest of tests. Adversity has given them advantage over those of us who have been going for the soft options. They have experienced frustrations and failure many times over, but were able to rise and move on. As the Chinese say it, 'The gem cannot be polished without friction, nor man perfected without trials'. For you to get to shine, you have to take on challenges coming your way, deal with them so that you get to find answers to your problems and take steps towards achieving your goals. Without a lot of pressure and heat there will be no diamond. The softer and lesser treatment only gives us the lesser minerals.

People who take risks are the people
you will always lose against.

Are you aware that from the same plant remains, you

can either get coal or diamond? Lower temperatures and pressure gives you coal. You only have to increase the heat and increase the pressure, over time and you will get diamond.

Had the vegetation been exposed to only mild treatment it will have changed to be compost, appreciated and admired by only a few who make direct use of it - agricultural use. This represent those of us who drift through life facing only the smallest of challenges, becoming adept at avoiding difficult situations. We will definitely be remembered for our usefulness but rarely our brilliance. A little more exposure to great heat and pressure will give a slightly more valuable coal. This will be those who face some tough times but soon give up. They have experience which makes them more valuable than those who never failed at anything. They nevertheless, lacked the staying power that could have made them reach the ultimate.

The precious diamond has been through it all. To see it, you will think it has been through an easy time, yet it has not. It has been through the ultimate test through time. People found at the very top did not get there overnight either. We see a product tested through time by the toughest of trials.

It is when you face problems that you discover things about yourself that you never really knew. Every problem you face brings you closer to understanding the real you. If you find yourself still not giving up after three failures in a given undertaking, you can consider yourself leadership material in your chosen field. Stay with it. That is, provided every time you fail, you learn something that puts you at a higher level. Indeed, after every fall, you rise to be at a level higher than when you started. It is not the material things that you use to show that you are growing, but the inner person who grows. Your actions following any failure are what is used to show how much you have grown.

In every crisis,there is a message. Crises are natures way of forcing change - breaking down old structures, shaking loose those negative habits so that something new and better can take their place. - Susan Taylor

---

It is not the things that happen to you that are important, but what you become through their influence. A true leader is inspired by failure not subdued by it. Should you find yourself running in another direction looking for yet another scheme to give a try, it is time to revise your purpose.

You are the sum total of all your experiences - your education, acquired skills plus your abilities lead to the real you. No other person can do what your can all because only you can put to use what you have learned and skills you acquired over the years. All you need is to knuckle down and be prepared to learn from all your experiences.

14

Procrastination - a thief of time

If only I had acted . . . . If only I had known . . . . If
only I had . . . . If only . . . . Hindsight always comes
too late. Often, when you have time, you may think
it is too soon, or you may unconsciously think, 'if I
wait long enough it will go away'; or 'there'll be time
enough in the future to take care of it'. Only when it
is late do you realize there is nothing much you can
do any more. It is then that you realize there is not
time enough to do what you thought could be done, it
is too late for it to have the effect it could have had.
In some cases it may have been overtaken by events,
and can no longer be done by yourself as others have
taken your place.

By procrastinating you lose out on what you could
have done; something, which if done promptly could

have led to achieving great result. Failure to act can
only lead to regrets.

Two people may, at the same time dream of doing
a similar project. For one, the dream dies away in the
face of all the supposedly insurmountable obstacles
that could be foreseen. Yet, the other person, faced
with a similar situation goes ahead to make the dream
work. The answer may lie with having both thought of
something that has not yet been tried, one person was
able to go right ahead and carried out whatever was
thought of. The other person continued to wait for the
right conditions, which seemed never to come. Regrets
will run along the lines of, 'if only I had ignored all
the wrong advices I got', or 'if only I had set time
aside to do what I thought was right', and many other
reasons which at the time seemed valid but have since
lost credibility. It is the one who acted on the vision
who made it.

When you belief more in what you could do you procrastinate less. That is if you are feeling like whatever you do is self-determined you get to be 'vital' and vigorous, lively and animated. This in turn diminishes the tendency to fear failure.

Our choice of friends at times become a source of regret. We spend time planning what to do, we listen to each other's advice. Some so called friends never take time to think of what is best for you, they only live for the now as they satisfy what is important to them. Often this comes in the form of shortlived successes as you do what is expected of you.

A good friend always gives good advice, even if they risk your anger. Friendship is about facing the good and overcoming the bad together. All emotions that can gather you and lift you up are pure and that emotion which seizes only one side of your being and so distorts you is impure.

When you choose to follow others blindly you ignore yourself and live only for them, you work to fulfil their purpose and goals, but never yours; you betray who you are and instead accept a fictional substitute as defined by your external environment. When you are externally oriented, you become helpless when others do not applaud you. Choose your friends well and have good people to help bring balance into life.

The friends you choose and what you do together will determine your future.

A human mind is fertile ground capable of producing a variety of fruit. Where you allow just any seed to fall on it and grow, it will grow wild. It is those who choose useful seeds and plant them that will reap useful harvest. A garden that is allowed to grow wild will continue to produce an abundance of wild seed. Take time to feed your mind good ideas and develop good habits. The good skills acquired will be useful in helping you act promptly and reliably.

Sometimes regrets are borne out of originally good intentions such as making the best of yourself. You get busy persuing your dream, which at the time means a lot to you and will bring personal fulfilment when realised. This may show itself as a tangible and real achievement visible to all. You get busy making big money, or busy gaining fame or simply succeeding in the course of your chosen career. Much later, when you are comfortable with what you wanted, you then realise that past friendships, your children, your spouse and all the people you love were also growing without you. They have now become strangers. You seem to be bound to them by relation only. It is only then that you realise you no longer have common ground to share. Too late you regret not having learnted to work and still be able to play with people who matter to you.

Growing children need to spend quality time with parents. To them, you are forever needed until they learn to do with less of you. And it is your children who decide when that would be. Teenagers find it difficult to start learning to be with a parent who could not reach them in their formative years. They would by then have found ways of replacing you in their emotional life as such you have become unnecessary. You can no longer be a source of advice or give parental guidance even when you think it is needed.

Life is what is happening while
we are busy making friends,
building careers, or just chilling.

There will be regrets for failing to do what you were supposed to do, when you were to do it, and realizing, often too late, that you could have done it. With hindsight you become aware that you could have had time to do what you had to, and all you failed to do was create opportunity to "do". Remember to always do what you have to do when it is to be done. You prepare well for your future by using your time well. There is no making up for wasted time, it stay lost.

Get out there and do your part. By procrastinating you delay taking your rightful place in order of things. Every moment counts, use it well to make the best of your life.

15

The inescapable state of mind

We all experience fear at one time or the other. Although when a child is born it does not 'know' fear, it will grow to experience fear. Soon fear becomes a part of our being. In fact, it can be considered that fear is part of the human condition. Fear is an emotion that is useful to us because in one way it can timely alert us of danger and therefore enable us to protect ourselves. You taking appropriate action to avert or minimize the possible danger's harmful effect can make the self-protection effective. In another way, fear can set in when we anticipate pain or something evil happening to us. Although fear is a vital response to physical and emotional danger, the response to fear could be crippling if we give in to it, living in a state of anxiety, worrying endlessly and simply being terrified and do nothing to address the source of fear. So, whether the threat is real or imagined you could give in to being afraid or get rid of fear by attending to the source of it.

For any individual to take a journey in life, we need to understand this most devastating emotion of fear. Fear can hold you back, fear can save you, and fear can educate you. Let us look at a scary thought and how to change the thought. Over the years I learned that some people tried to manage fearful emotion by using drugs, but they failed. They continue to be afraid to the point of being destroyed by the drugs in an attempt to drown the fear. Abusive husbands and wives attack their spouses but fail to rid themselves of the fear. The abuse does not wipe away the fear. It may even make the fear grow as the 'paranoia' of the mistrust increases. Someone brandishing a gun continues to experience fear though may have picked the gun hoping it will make them less afraid. The list is endless. All we need to do is follow how the mind works as it experiences fear and start thinking about how to address it so that it does not involve you in a spiral of crippling actions that can stop your growth.

If you pause and reason around and about 'the fear' you experience at any moment, you get to learn why you get it, how to positively handle it such that you grow. Fear not controlled can hold you back and stop you achieving your goals.

We all are afraid of and worry about different things. Some could even seem small and inconsequential to those who are not directly affected. Previous bad experiences or traumas can trigger a fear response within us that is hard to quell. The only way to get past such demons is to face them. Lower their intimidating effects by breaking them down into parts so that you put up a proper plan of action to handle them.

When you are afraid, your mind can build different scenarios that stress the importance of the fear. Before you know it that fear cripples you.

What is it that you are afraid of? Is it a possible 'no' to a particular request or for a job application? For as long as you do not know whether that 'no' will come or not you will remain afraid. To overcome this fear, do what you have to do first - act on it. Go ahead and apply for the job. If you think you lack skills to do the job that is what you have to work on.

Overcome fear through employing a healthy self-talk. Think and talk yourself into action. Once you start an activity, it becomes less frightening than before. Action overcomes fear.

Get your advice from the right people. Those who have actually done what you want to do – the people who have taken the journey before you are best placed to tell you how it is done.

When you take action - doing what you fear or are afraid of, your worries are minimized or will disappear completely and you are left with a feel of euphoria, a feeling of exhilaration that gives you confidence to go on. The excitement is not necessarily a result of having succceded, for it will be there even if you did not. Your mind is less occupied with having not acted. It is simply a result of having made a decision and having been able to get an answer to a concern.

The best way to stop worrying is to start solving the problem that is worrying you.

Fear distorts and gives an inaccurate picture of situations and events. When you are afraid and do not act, you fail to establish what exactly you are afraid of. You will find yourself running away from something that is not after you. If then you base your future on such fears, you are using a distorted and inaccurate guideline.

Fear makes one stay in an abusive relationship for years without realizing there is something they can do to get out. It may be fear of being alone that makes you believe that you are worth nothing when you are on your own. Yet, that particular relationship may be dragging you down, reducing you to insignificant levels. It is only when you act and talk yourself out of it that you begin to realize that you deserve more than you are getting. Only then can you move on to something better.

Fear teaches one to act only when there is guarantee for success; it makes one see danger where there is none; anticipate disaster where there is supposed to be hope.

To give in to your fears is to surrender to suppressive forces; it is like you are quietly crawling into oblivion. You give up the chance to live and breathe success.

Until you confront your fears, you will never experience the freedom to achieve great things.

It is easy to do the same old things even if we know they are unsatisfactory than to try new ideas. It takes tremendous inner strength to act different from what we normally do in order to change the realities of our lives.

The unknown manifests itself in a number of different ways to different people. At one level it may represent not having had a chance to be exposed to different ways of doing things, such that you avoid anything that is unfamiliar. This is failing to try out new ideas or failing to face challenges in ways that you have not experienced before.

Fear of the unknown also leads to procrastinating when you are delaying to act even when you are dissatisfied with the present situation. You may be aware of what you have to do but you are not acting. Day in and day out you are comfortable doing the things you are familiar with, those that you have been doing time and again. Even when you are aware that things are not working well for you and you should try something new, you keep on postponing and promising yourself you will try something else soon, only to find that soon never comes. Often, you find yourself putting it off to another time. That will not do. You know what you want to do; all that you need is the courage to put it in place.

Nothing will ever change for
you, until you change.

It is our fears that prevent us from trying out new ideas, and doing what has never been done, despite knowing it will bring better rewards. Nothing grows on ice. If you let tradition freeze your mind, new ideas cannot sprout. Traditional thinking freezes the mind. It prevents it from developing creative powers. The unknown represent opportunities that await you to discover.

Fear prevents us from experiencing the thrill of facing a challenge and winning no matter what it takes. This is where we are afraid of failing and being labelled failures. Often, we fear losing what we already have in case one has to give it up to do something new. Then rationalizing comes in. You begin to be content with what you are – after all you are earning better than some people and live in a better house, drive a reasonable car, etc. The fear of failure often stops us from taking action. You may do so because you are afraid of being ridiculed, criticized or being laughed at by others if you fail. Understand that your failing or your succeeding is all your doing. It may be easier to succeed having done something than failing as a result of not trying at all. Failure, no matter how often it is experienced can be looked upon as a bridge, it acts as a point where you pause to determine how to proceed. Allowing fear in at such a time makes failure a barricade to success.

Fear makes real that which never was.

Self-doubt creeps in if you lack faith in your ability to achieve what you dream. You may even compare yourself against others whom you will be thinking are better than you. 'If they could not make it, who am

I to ever imagine I could do better?' Yet you are not aware why they failed. Better still, you are yourself, with special talents and potential which need not be restricted on the basis of what other people are able to or not able to do.

The fear of insecurity makes us cautious and eventually we surrender and settle for what we have now.

To allow fear to direct your ways is to worry yourself into inaction. To fight fear, you have to learn to bring your attention to the present. Take note of what you have now, your state of health, your finances and current earnings, and your skills. Think of ways of dealing with each of your concerns in the best way possible. Take advantage of your strengths; use the positives in your life to move on to better things.

Fear cripples the mind, and all reasonable thoughts slowly die away.

Do not let fear control your life. Learn ways of handling fear that will enable you to move forward – learning from the moment, acting to solve a problem and freeing your mind to engage in more useful activities to less anxiety.

What joy is there in excelling at nothing? It is better to try something and fail than never knowing if you have it in you to do better.

Learn to face things as they are and not make excuses. It is then that you will be able to celebrate your success because you know that you rightly deserve it. Come to terms with your shortcomings; do not dwell on them nor let them limit you. Learn to compensate for your weaknesses and do not apologize for them. Excuses merely take away your right to fail, as such giving up your right to grow and face life with dignity.

There is no problem that can ever be greater than you. As you look for and act in ways that lead to overcoming challenges you face, your creative side will kick-in to come up with good ideas to deal with it. All you have to do is to take the plunge, have the guts to try out something new, even if you risk being hurt in the process. There is no success without risk.

Do what you are afraid to do; go where you are afraid to go; when you run away because you are afraid to do something big, you give up the opportunity to learn. Face your fears, and death of fear is guaranteed.

16

Silent sabotage

When one is faced with a challenge and they strongly believe they can overcome it, often they are able to find ways that allow them to do just that. This is the power of self-belief. To achieve any goal in life, you must believe you are going to be successful. If you do not, you are likely to fail. If you take time to follow through on why you fail at something even when you are determined to succeed you are likely to find that somehow you are silently sabotaging yourself. It is this silent self-sabotaging tendency that we all have to overcome and strongly belief in self to get ahead.

All people have goals and would like to succeed in life. Some make a lot of effort to research into their area of interest. Yet, they may fail to take the necessary step to get to realize their desired goal. I had for a long time wanted to be a writer. I worked hard at putting some material together. I kept on writing bits and pieces about what I intended but did not really collate it and come up with a book. Many years later, after some soul searching, I realized it was mainly because I did not believe that the book would be good enough for other people to want to read. Self-doubt was telling me that there are a lot of other books out there that are better than what I could ever produce. I did not believe that I could be a successful writer. The time I got round to compiling my first book was when I reversed the self-doubt into self-belief. 'Someone, somewhere out there, will pick my book and benefit from what I have to say'. 'If I was able to imagine that I have something good to share, then it must be good'. These kind of thoughts were enough to give me the courage to get on with what I intended. You too can do anything you put your mind to. Only self-doubt can stop you.

Nothing good ever happens unless you believe in yourself - what you can do for yourself or others as well as believing in the good others can do. Take a moment think back over some of the things you have tried and failed to achieve over the last few years. It can also be you have thought of something and you never went ahead to do anything about. Ask yourself if when you started on your goal you really believed you would succeed. Chances are you will find that you didn't really believe you could make it. It is vital that you take steps to make sure that your self-belief remains strong at all times to ensure that you achieve your goals.

Winners take risks and are willing to live with the consequences.

Self-belief without action will not get you very far. You have to make a proper plan of action which in the beginning while your confidence to do what you have to may still be low will provide the routine that will keep you going. Inform yourself so that you have the working knowledge and skills for what you want. Even with the strongest determination, you cannot make a success of any venture without skills. If you want to be a writer you have to develop writing skills. Practice writing even if it is short stories not necessarily related to what you intend to write about, keep a diary where you note detail about your daily experiences, volunteer to write minutes in meetings, improve your observation skills to bring objectivity to what you write, etc. consult with other writers, be a reader yourself to experience what other writer do or have to say, take a writing course. All the things you do will be directed at acquiring skills related to what you want to do. Nothing you have to do is too small. Everything adds to skills build-up you will need to do what you have to well. Whatever you want to do write it down prominently in you notebook. Start listing what you have to do to close knowledge and skills gap. Then go right ahead to work on it.

Know your strengths and go on a deliberate program to maximize what you can do. Raw talent is wasted if you do not discipline yourself to work on perfecting it so that it works for you. Gold winning athletes work hard to perfect their skills for major events. Yet, even after breaking all records, that is personal and those of others, they still keep practicing to get even more out of themselves. They know that today's success is tomorrow's mediocre performance. If you dwell too long on your today's performance you stop yourself from winning another gold in the future. Push yourself to the limit at all times then you will not fall short of doing your best in each day.

No matter how good your intentions to be successful, you silently sabotage yourself when you allow yourself to dwell too long in your comfort zone and not venture into the unknown. You limit yourself to doing only what you know or what others have done before you. You do not allow your creativity to guide you into new areas. Innovate and allow yourself the pleasure of creating new records, as well as providing your community and clients a new service.

We all need the help of others to achieve our goals. This could be in the form of direct input where they guide or coach, it could be by collaborating with others for mutual benefit. To work as a team means recognizing that we are different people, each with special talents and we can each uniquely contribute towards the final goal. No team ever reaches its potential until each member does and, have this coordinated towards a common goal. By failing to take advantage of available resources and not playing your role as you should, you limit and even prevent your own success.

We tend to beat ourselves when we allow our

fears to rule our actions. Knowing you are good at something, but letting others take the responsibility of deciding for you how you can use your talent is the beginning of failing to fulfil your potential.

We each of us have a place where we can add most value. Know your strengths and start using them to advantage.

When you fear criticism, you become economical at taking risks, it is like defending in a game without making efforts to score. You want to make sure that nothing will happen that will show you in a bad light. It is when you venture to take risks that somewhere in there something good would come of it. You will lose some and surely be criticised for it, but the joy of winning a few will outweigh the momentary embarrassments. You will even develop the taste for winning and get to want to try out new things knowing you will learn from mistakes made. The euphoria experienced after winning is addictive. Once you get used to winning you constantly set out to look for ways to win.

Winners take risks and are willing to
live with the consequences.

When the desire to succeed is great, we assert ourselves both mentally and physically to give peak performance. We are quick to make decisions and see them through by taking appropriate action. We become more aware that mistakes made help us to learn more about what we intend to achieve. You become instrumental to your success when you give yourself permission to succeed. Only you can get rid of all the silent self-sabotaging tendencies and let positive self-belief through. Any time the best of you wins it adds to your self-confidence and it is the motivation you need to keep going up.

17

Position yourself and take responsibility

No matter what happens, remember to always keep both your heart and head above the water. Remain positive and optimistic. Be proactive rather than give in to prevailing circumstances hoping things will work themselves out.

You cannot change the past but you can set things in motion that will influence the future.

No ship can successfully go on a journey without the proper working compass and skillful, knowledgeable crew to traverse the oceans. You are the captain of your ship. You have to direct your life's journey. You are responsible for what happens to it both from inside and outside. The ship (you life) has to face nature's tempests – the challenges that relentlessly hit on you; crew's mutiny – your moments of weakness when you confidence crumbles, your skills not holding up and not being well informed on what you have to do, etc. Position yourself so that you are ready, well prepared to take charge of your life. Otherwise you risk outright failure, as you will be unlikely to hold up to all the challenges.

- Identify and map out you journey's route – you dreams and vision and plans to get there.
- Prepare well for the journey – knowledge, skills and competencies that will see you through the journey.
- Build resilience and stay on your route – you will win some on this journey and lose some. Use any failures you experience to learn what to do better.
- Enjoy the journey – celebrate your successes and use these to set up for even more and better.

Your present state of life need not be the final. You can change it if you dare to try. Things never work themselves out, they need you to act. You cannot wait patiently in the face of a trying situation and hope for a miraculous intervention which never comes. Instead, act. It may be in what you say or in what you do. Small though it may seem, it might make a world of difference to those around you or to what you intend it for. Nothing is predestined to work without your input.

Learn not to always accept things as they are handed out to you. Otherwise you only get another person's wishes or expectations. Make your own tracks. Do what will enable you to look back and see your footprints and not be confused with those of others - innovate.

Make each day special by thinking of something special for it. Do or say on that day that which will add to its uniqueness. In this way you create a positive environment within you.

You tend to be held back by what you think you are not - your belief that you are not good enough, not knowledgeable enough, not worthy enough.

The difference between a successful person and an average person is in the way each of them handles rejection and failure. Champions learn from defeat and it is often a very humbling experience to face a great player who has just experienced defeat. An average player always comes forth as the underdog, and may even make it look like it is their due to be defeated by one and all. The difference between the two is that a winner does not use past history as a measure of what is going to happen. Winners learn from all that they have gone through and will face the new situation just as that - a new situation. The other person may have very little past experience to learn from and as such is clueless what to do in the circumstances.

Great people learn more from personal
defeat or failure than from their successes.

Whatever struggles you go through, learn by them it will pay off in the long run. Great people reflect and pay attention to all the circumstances surrounding their failure or success, then use what they learn to map out a new course of action.

Success is not an accident. You relentlessly work at it. Often as you succeed at something you are more likely to take it for granted and even fail to realize that the success experienced may have been temporary. Just like in failure, success requires that you continue to find ways to improve on what you have for you to continue to do well. Success is never 'done'. It is something you continue to work on for you to keep improving.

We are the sum total of the choices
and decisions we make everyday.

Life is a journey, and yours started way back when you were born. This journey will end some day in death. In between the two dates is the period that is entirely in your hands. You can turn it into a sorry state – time wasted mourning your misfortunes, time spent in apprehension and fear of life after death and many other ills, a time when you receive from others and actively please yourself in unrewarding ways. It can also turn out to be a period for experiencing growth in all areas of your life: family, social, spiritual and professional, time for experiencing joy of creating

and building monuments and landmarks of success.
Your success story need not end when your life ends.
Those who actively create leave footprints that those
left behind will remember forever.

18

The journey of a thousand miles
begins with one step

You have your dreams, desires and goals, and you may have your plans (or lack thereof) of achieving them. The journey to reach your destination is an odorous one and it is possible that you could give up without going the distance. To go on the journey of life is a no nonsense undertaking. No one can live or run your life for you if you are to achieve goals that are specifically yours. You need to learn and acquire your own experiences; develop skills how you handle the many chores and experiences of life. In the process you develop competencies that will enable you to handle your journey with efficiency, making you effective.

Your attitudes, habits and skills are the assemblage of qualities that become your tools of choice.

Specifically, we cannot go far without relevant competencies. These we achieve as we actively work on our goals acquiring skills. Learning new skills makes you capable and your confidence goes up. It is important to realize that gaining new skills is one sure way of growing, preparing yourself for venturing into any field confidently. Acquisition of necessary skills builds your competency and with that you can follow your dreams.

Being skilled makes you capable and enables you to efficiently complete tasks. Your abilities and competencies make it possible for you to stand someplace that you can call your personal space. By making your life count you call the shots in your life – giving your life direction, efficiently working for what you want and effectively using your time as you attend to your responsibilities. Those who keep increasing their skills and competencies become better and better at handling challenges they face, and by being able to do so grow in experience. Teach yourself to increase your experience at everything you do. Avoid staying too long at the same thing. Repeated experience with one thing year after year shows you are stagnating. It may be the beginning of the declining quality as your time is no longer being used efficiently, you are sitting too long at the same level and may be missing out on new ways to make your life count.

Acquire the knowledge base, skills and experiences that will push you in the right direction. Skills will give you the competency to achieve your ultimate dream.

Opportunities come your way in different forms and from any direction. One such opportunity came to me by chance when someone contacted and invite me to what she then called a special meeting. I got to learn it was about a multi-level marketing opportunity. The concept of network marking inspired me and brought change in my life. I believe the work of networking with people is by far the best in developing skills and sharing the struggle on the journey to success.

No matter when in the stage of your life, be open to embrace opportunities. The book of life is not written in stone. We each of us write our own story. Be alert and on the look out for yours. Learn from every moment and keep growing. Make sure you grow in proportion to the time you spend on whatever you do. Never stop growing mentally even if the physical grow stops.

Your life journey – from birth to death, needs you to keep it vibrant and interesting. The joy of living that brings you happiness and contentment means you will be living your life on your term. Whatever that is inscribed as your journey is your choice. No amount of excuses can ever be acceptable as adequate and appropriate explanation for short-changing yourself. We all require 'the courage to be' and our wellbeing depends on moving forward with this courage so that you get to live a fulfilled life, and you are responsible for what your life becomes.

www.ingramcontent.com/pod-product-compliance
Lightning Source LLC
Chambersburg PA
CBHW060117120726
48003CB00009B/2674